22 DAYS

AROUND THE COAST OF BRITAIN

(or the Earl Grey Tea Coast)

NICK SANDERS

Photography by Ian Woollams

Designed by David Moss

Production by D.J.M Graphics Studio Bryan Blakeborough
Phototypesetting by Gallireed Ltd., Stalybridge. Printed by Heanor Gate Printing Ltd., Heanor. Binding by Sherratts of Manchester.
Published by Nicholas Sanders Publishing Ltd., P.O. Box 17, Glossop, Derbyshire, SK13 8AX.

© Nick Sanders, September 1984
ISBN 0 946940 03 7 (case bound)

It might at first seem strange attempting to 'explore' a country as developed as Britain. Exploration is normally thought of as discovering a new pygmy tribe in the Congo, or shooting the rapids down the Sunkosi River. Having biked around the world and journeyed in crazy and exotic places, I was genuinely excited about journeying to places in the land where I was born. After all, I thought, I'd been to Kathmandu, but I'd never been to Cornwall – or Scotland, for that matter.

I have always maintained that the essence of exploration is the attitude within. A trip to the dark side of the moon needs little in the way of assistance to ignite the imagination; but what about brash Blackpool, deserted northern Scotland, Scarborough or Eastbourne? There is as much to discover about tough, good-humoured Liverpool as there is about the Sudan. Of course, writing about my **Journey to the Source of the Nile** was easier than **22 Days** because fewer people go to the 'source' than go to Bognor Regis, so how could I be disputed?!

For this reason, I hope that **22 Days Around the Coast of Britain** will be accessible to more people. Perhaps the fleeting first impressions which rush by in a jumble should be read only as that. Travel can only be understood when one is on the move. Stopping to explore in depth usually means interrupting the journey and that I didn't want to do.

The 22 day record ride was not my main consideration in the whole project, but any act of originality, however slight, I think is worth doing.

Glossop
England
August 1984

There are various ways of travelling and even more reasons for the same, but if you're travelling for pleasure and you wartt, in travelling, to find out something more about the country you are travelling through than you would from a car window then there's no better way than by foot or on a bicycle.

Walking and cycling take you through the world at a human pace at a timbre that relates directly back to you as a person. How fast can you go? How fast do you want to go?

I've done both and I think that for isolation and freedom walking beats them all, while for covering the ground a little faster yet still covering it at a human pace cycling has the fine edge.

I believe too that when you're travelling you take yourself with you – a simplistic statement and one that may seem ridiculous too but one that nevertheless I believe. If you travel trying to escape from or find yourself then you're a fool because whatever you see, whoever you meet, you meet head on with all the myriad of impressions and feelings that went into the making of you. A sour man looks on the world sadly, a content man sees it in a different light.

This is by way of bringing me round to the point of this foreword. I first met Nick Sanders when I cycled with him out of Lancashire towards the Yorkshire Dales. He's not a very ordinary person, nobody who cycles round the world, to the foothills of the Himalayas and then to the source of the Nile could be, but his outlook on life and his openness in his meetings with people as well as his questioning of himself and his own motives in travelling make him a welcome fireside companion for anyone who like me is as much an armchair explorer as the real thing.

In his book you can travel round the coastline of Britain with Nick in two ways. Firstly in a leisurely and quixotic way with Nick meeting seaside landladies and the many many English eccentrics that make this such a strange nation, secondly you can gallop along with him at lung-bursting, Vimto-guzzling speed on his world record breaking ride, following in his own wheel tracks, enjoy it!

Mike Harding

Dad, on Dartmoor, spring 1940, aged 26

To My Father

As soon as I returned from Africa last year having journeyed to the source of the Nile, I immediately started thinking about the next project. I wanted to go to South America and follow the Andes to Tierra del Fuego, or maybe even adventure in the States. It seemed inevitable, though that after three years of travelling out of the country I should journey nearer home. Britain sounded parochial at first, but before long I realised just how difficult it would be.

The first thing to do was to mark out the route and decide how to embark on the journey. I wanted to write about a slow amble, but from every side it was suggested that I have a go at the world record. Why not do both? The Guiness Book of Records said it was a simple matter of following the nearest tarmacadamed road to the coast. That turned out to be just under 5,000 miles and I reckoned that 21 days (Day 1 to Day 22) would give me a daily mileage of around 230 to 240 miles each day. If I was going to make a new record, then I wanted it to be respected.

Discussing the project with my sponsors Vimto, John Nichols, the Marketing Director, seemed to like the general concept and the

company agreed to continue their support. The preparations could begin. Initially I was training 300 miles a week; five months later it was 90 miles a day. I spent a lot of time in the gym working on the upper body; nothing could be left to chance or underestimated.

Press Secretary Vivienne handled all the publicity, an enormous task which was absolutely essential to the success of the project. I was to phone Viv several times a day so she could tie up meetings with the local media around the country, accounting perhaps for two hours valuable cycling time a day.

Cycling at 15 m.p.h. even in the hills meant at least 15 continuous hours in the saddle. I was obviously going to need a back-up team. Barry was to look after everything from the driving to the navigation to arranging meal and rest stops.

Photographs for the book had to be taken on the journey and Ian, the photographer who met me at the source of the Nile, agreed to come along.

So all was set, all I needed was good weather without too many head winds and a hope that I would sleep well and barring accidents was quietly confident.

All the food and equipment needed to
support the 22 day journey.

ACKNOWLEDGEMENTS

The Bicycle
Harry Hall Framesets 22" (39" 73°)
Specialized Equipment: Gear Ratio
44, 52 x 13, 14, 15, 16, 17, 18, 19.

The Clothes
Jerseys, Gibbsport, Salford.
Tracksuits, Le Coq Sportif, Holmes Chapel.
Shoes, Sidi of Italy.

The Cameras
2 Nikon F.3's, Nikon UK Ltd.
1 Nikon FM
24mm, 35mm, 50mm, 75 – 150mm, 300mm.
Kodakchrome 64 Etkachrome 200.
(courtesy of Stockport Express)

The Food
Vimto, J.N. Nichols, Manchester.
Shredded Wheat, Nabisco
Peanut Butter, Sunpat Products, Hadfield.

The Accommodation
Scotland, Karrimor Camping, Accrington.
England, kind assistance from the English Tourist Board.

The Training
Herriots Leisure Centre, Manchester.

The Team
*Special thanks to Ian Woollams for working so hard on the
photographs and Barry Duckworth, team driver and official
food taster for keeping me sane. To Viv Bouchier for translating
my frantic jibberish to the press and for helping hold the project together. Dave Moss for his patience and enthusiasm in
putting the book together. To John Clowes for telling me what
paragraphs are, Jane Bannister for helping me with my groping
words, and Pete Dean for reconstructing my sentences!
To Mike Harding for a lovely foreword. Thanks also to my
sponsors. And lastly, to my eccentric dad for always being
there, my love.*

Twenty two hours in a phone
box? A lot of valuable cycling
time will be lost this way.

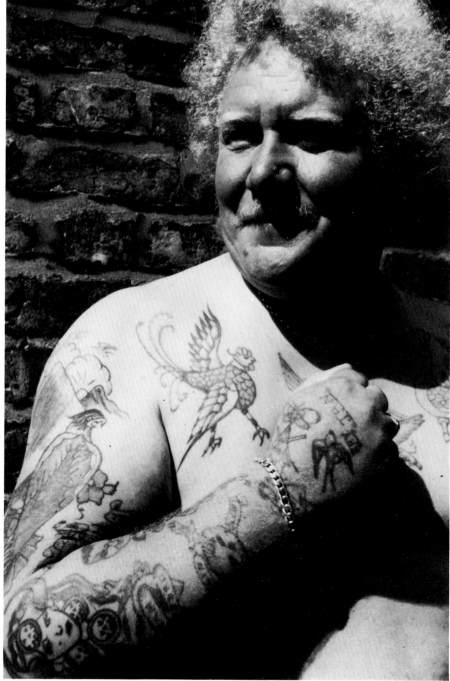

Two lovers kiss on the beach; it's windy and it's cold and the sea is faraway. Lovers in Blackpool complain there's nowhere to go, until they find the beach.

Turning away to look along the promenade I felt transfixed, immobilised by my first ever awareness of the passing of time in one huge chunk. It was twenty years since I'd scampered in the sand with a bucket and spade, a piece of sticky rock and half-a-crown a day for spends.

An off-season Saturday afternoon in Blackpool is cold and windy and wet and dull and two lovers snog on the sands. It's a funny word 'snogging' . . . like slogging or hogging and the meaning we instil into the word is like a grope in the dark. So too, there's something invisible about lovers caught in romance that's raw all over and blue at the fingertips. The back row of the cinema perhaps; a littered door or a backstreet alley; on the beach, on the prom, on the hoof, on the run. A dog barks at their heels and children kick a leather football against the promenade wall. No-one seems to care.

Blackpool has always been a haven for forlorn, wistful factory folk looking out to sea in the face of monotony and uniformity; the small traders of Lancashire belching against a strong Atlantic wind. And as the green and squeaky trams trundle towards the tower I felt like an old man who talks about his life as if it were yesterday, not realising that another ten years had just swiftly passed by.

Seagulls float against the wind. The great black-backed gull and his great greedy belly. Steeped in stolen fish heads their only salvation is the charm of their early morning cries to start a journey by the sea.

"Are you riding in the milk race then"? said Ken, the proprietor of a small bed and breakfast on Clifton Road. "I entered the wife last year", he chuckled as he went back into the kitchen.

Ken was a Welshman with a searching, intimidating glass eye. Glass eyes, like snogging, are anachronisms which embarrass because of their obviousness. Something to laugh at but not talk about. Like class consciousness, much too obvious to be of any use to anyone.

I'd missed dinner (dinner amalgamated with afternoon tea at 5 pm so Ken could watch the 'tele') but he made me a cup of coffee. Maureen, his wife was grossly pregnant and nearly four foot wide. "I'll rub your belly luv", said Ken, "I'm nearer to it than you". The combined weight of mother and daughter was precisely one fifth of a ton.

An elderly couple sat down next to me, Mr & Mrs Wighton. They once cycled from Edinburgh to London to watch Randulph Turpin beat Sugar Ray Robinson. "Marvellous fight; nothing like it since", said Mr Wighton, and a life-time's collection of gold lucky charms clinked wearily on his wife's podgy arms.

"I read biographies you know; I've read Charles Bronson. He came from a family of 14 children, his brother's a drop-out in New York". She hardly paused for a breath, only to peer at me, wondering. "Do you like drop-outs"? said Mrs Wighton, clutching a bead of her pearl necklace. "Maybe I am one", I said. "Go 'er way, yer hair 'aint long enough". But she turned away all the same.

On the small dining-room wall plastered with a white polyfilla compound, a 'genuine' and original Sudanese spear hung alongside a set of reproduction leather skin brown bongo drums. The coat-of-arms of a Blackpool landlady. Stay out until 4 pm, stay in after 11 pm; no smoking in the rooms. No women, no men, no dogs or cats or dirty books and you wake up at the sound of carpet slippers and a tarry clearing of a morning throat.

This was the first time I'd ever stayed in a bed and breakfast; over the next few months I'd never be out of one. I said goodbye as Ken asked me if I'd like Maureen along for fun and I politely declined.

The sun was shining but the westerly breeze was cold. On the North Pier the inflatable cinema advertised 'The Twelve Minute Thrill Show'. Hardly worth bothering, I thought, but apparently it's the excitation of a lifetime. And the Rock King sells sticky, messy, world famous Blackpool rock. And Derek the tatooist needles affectations, ramblings to mother on broad muscular biceps. And Angelina Petulengo tells you what you want to know in front of Mr B's amusement arcade. A megaphone calls out 'come along inside and have a wonderful time NOW' to the tune of the forced laughter of funland.

The noise and the fun on the prom in the sun and two more lovers embrace on the beach by a cloudy sea. Maybe they're the same ones as last night on a marathon session practising for the grand occasion . . . whatever that might be.

In sight of the Tower a young fellow leaned his bike against mine and sat down in a cafe next to me. "Are you a writer"? he said.

"Sort of . . . " I carried on scribbling a few notes.

"Thought so", he said, "'cos I am as well". His accent was a deep rich Mancunian. It was a coincidence. "I want to write for the Daily Mirror, you know. Kief Waterhouse, you know, he's great in't he"?

I said that I'd heard of him. Had he heard of Paul Theroux?

"Paul la Rue? Wot a stupid name, never 'erd of 'im". I told him he was a famous travel writer who wrote for the Sunday Times.

"Tuff", he said, getting stuck into the plate of chips he'd ordered, "that's 'is fault innit; bet I know more people who don't know 'im than you do who do". I couldn't deny that, but I bet the only people he knew were his mates, the landlord of his local pub and the names of all the breweries in the north of England. "Anyway, I bet he writes for posh people like you, they always do".

Away from his environment his working class defences were up. He argued until he was red in the face that it was better to be working class and poor than to to be 'well to do' and have to talk 'posh'. 'Posh' in his terms was anyone who didn't talk in a broad colloquial dialect. He was called Kev and talking to him made the outskirts of Blackpool just that bit more exciting. It was still cloudy and the sea was still and dead when two pretty Blackpool girls walked past.

"Hey, luv, come over 'ere. I'll give you some ice cream". One of the girls turned round in amazement at this throw-up of Industrial Man. "They're a bit tasty, aint they"? His eyes bulged out of his very red face. He had short, curly black hair and the sort of honest face that would sell you a used car with only twenty miles of life left. His face had the sort of dark red colouration that indicates high blood pressure and whenever he got excited his flaccid cheeks went patchy. "I cycled twenty miles the other day it was murder, last time you get me out on a bike". At that, he pulled out a small bottle of Lucozade and poured it over a grazed knee.

"Fell off me bike din' I? Aids recovery this, sez so on the bottle", and he swigged the little that was left. I eventually told him I was training to bike 220 miles a day around the coast and that meant doing the journey twice; once for the training, the second being the record ride.

"220 miles a day, you must be mad", he said, coughing on a chip, "why do you do it"?

I told him that even I thought such journeying was ludicrous, but that one reason why I did it was because most other occupations were even more so.

"I like a good booze up. Get out wi me

mates, pick up some birds and give 'em some wellie . . . you don't know what yer missin". The number of "birds he'd pulled", after a bellyfull of ale, moves into double figures in front of beery pals. He'll stink now until morning and wake up coughing in a pile of sweat. Saturday afternoon is football on the television and a few more cans of Carlsberg. Saturday night is another picked at meat and potato pie. Sunday lunch gets another soaking which carries onto another 'do' with the lads at night. As a character he was as rough on the surface as a ton of millstone grit. But just occasionally he showed an inkling of another side to his character as he threw cold chips to gathering birds.

"You've got to feed 'em, aven't you"? he said, "I'll even buy you a cuppa if you like". As I got up to leave, a little ketchup dribbled down his chin and surplus Lucozade oozed out of his grazed knee. At least he wasn't bothered with calculated diplomacy and pretentious mannerisms.

A middle-aged fellow with a square-set

forehead and straight hair that fell over his eyes had followed me into the cafe and when Kev got up and left asked me what I was doing. We chatted and eventually when I'd finished he asked me if I'd like another tea at his place.

Sid Emery looked friendly and we walked back to his little pre-war bungalow. Immediately he opened the door I knew he was harmless and lonely. As he put an old whistling kettle on the stove I was amazed at the rich life he displayed.

The living room was lilac and faded and sitting on a green felt lined card table there was an old Remington typewriter, soft calf leather binoculars and a matchstick reproduction of Drakes Golden Hinde in a bottle. Above the table on the wall, barrels of polished wood had been lifted from various sections of famous ships. From the bowspit of H.M.S. Victory, Nelson's Flagship in 1805. Another barrel came from H.M.S. Restless, and another from the deck of the Mauritania. Sid was busying himself in the kitchen and I was trespassing in the heart and soul of someone else's life. There was a Picasso print of a mother suckling her child next to a sepia print of Nelson and copper kettles sat here and there in between more ships in bottles. And next to a rendition of Desiderata, Sid's own sea view oils leaned dustily on a replica quarter scale model Dutch organ. The kettle started to whistle and Sid brought in the tea. He didn't say much; I think he was pleased that some-one was interested in his curios.

"I supply fishing props to exhibitions, I do", he said at last, "Me lobster pots are famous they are; appeared in the 'Singing Postman' didn't they"? I didn't doubt it for a moment and I stared at a tatty old lobster basket feeling quite in awe.

"Me fishing nets were in Dr. Doolittle's and as for the boat show, well they wud awl come ta me, wouldn't they"?

Sid boasted this and stood by the mantlepiece looking with pride at his world famous lobster pots. And when he'd finished what he had to say, we said goodbye and he would lie in wait for his next captive audience of one to charm and share and show.

For all her sticky brashness, leaving Blackpool was like saying goodbye to a friend. If friendship is familiarity and familarity breeds contempt, then it's only one being unsure amidst the massive murmur and tinkling moans of a seaside town having a grand time.

Day 1

Blackpool

Had a lovely send off from the people of Blackpool. The official start was at the top of the tower; I wonder where the finish will be! It was really nice to see so many people turn up to see me off. I didn't know them but they said they knew me. BBC TV were there and Maddie, the director got a policeman to stop the traffic whilst the presenters Mark and Maggie stood by the tape. I wasn't apprehensive because to do nearly 250 miles a day requires complete confidence. After the film crew drift off so do the crowd.

On the A590 from Grange Over Sands.

A quick half hour break because of the hold up this morning. Ian's taking pictures of cows. Photographers are very strange people. Barry puts on his 'Don't Ask Me I'm Only The Driver' sweat shirt and already he tells me I've got to get going when all I want to do is sleep in the sun. Two large motorbikes ride past then accelerate into a wheelie at over 80mph. The bicycle feels so tame compared to that. Watching the cars zoom past on the duel carriageway towards Barrow I think it's so much nicer not being couped up in hot, tin boxes. Not that it's particularly easy on a bike.

Between Seascale and Eyemouth 7.25 pm

The road from Barrow can't have a flat section in it. I'm feeling a bit tired. First day blues. Hope tomorrow is easier. Ian's taking more pictures of more cows. Barry keeps tabs on the itinerary. "Well drag me over a blazing hot coal what have we got here". Apparently if I make it to Silloth tonight I'll have 45 miles in hand for tomorrow.

Silloth 10.00 pm

Arrived at the Solway Lido. Chalets, bungalows and caravans. We've got a caravan. Finished my shower and Barry's brought back a Chinese for three. "Good grub, a nice brew and a roof over our heads", he said and "who's pinched me soap"?

Blackpool – Silloth.

Liftman Stan and I going up in the world ... to the top of Blackpool Tower!

Cycling on to Cleveleys and then Fleetwood and then the pretty Pilling road, the smells of candy-floss, strawberry ice cream, hot popcorn and toffee apples became the steaming pungent piquancy of freshly laid cow pat. It wasn't long before I'd wound my way onto Lancaster and Lancaster seemed to be full of one-way streets and secondhand bookshops. No doubt there would be many an old first edition to discover; a Coleridge perhaps, or one of Burton's diaries. But it was Sunday and Lancaster was closed.

An old man walked towards me and I asked him if he knew of a tea shop, but he was only passing through, reminiscing, "I went to Lancaster Grammar School over 60 years ago", he said, "but I don't know it now".

He was a tall, well built, old man stooping slightly as old tall people are wont to do. His round national health specs were too tight as ever and gave his bulging eyes the look of a pervert. His black ankle length coat was frayed and tatty and he smelt. When I leaned towards him to speak he backed away; I suppose he thought I smelt too. All he clutched was a green plastic canvas bag containing a copy of the Sunday Express magazine and an umbrella. A packet of sandwiches perhaps, a spare pair of socks or maybe a dead rat would be disclosed as he clutched the bag tightly. I wanted to ask him where he was going and felt guilty when I did.

"Well I lived in Blackpool but the hooligans drove me out so now I travel; never stopped these last twenty years". As he scratched his white, stubbly chin he pulled out a pocket watch and I was Alice talking to the White Rabbit.

"Course I can't play the piano like I used to do", he said, thumbing his watch back into his waistcoat waiting for me to say 'oh really'.

"Oh really", I said. "How interesting".

"Yes, yes. I'm a classical pianist you might say, seven or eight hours a day, all of my life, Schumann, Chopin, Listz. Look, you've got to have very flexible fingers", and he showed me his hands. They were small, artistic, calloused and dirty. They most certainly weren't flexible.

Suddenly he pulled out his watch. Oh, my goodness, he said and his eyes bulged. "Got to go, I'm ever so late", and as much as an old man can, he scampered off around the corner and was gone.

Cycling along the four mile promenade at Morecambe I was well on my way to Carnforth, then on to Grange-over-Sands, genteel Victorian watering place, and round Morecambe Bay to Barrow-in-Furness. The image I had in my mind of Barrow, all docks and ship yard, made me wonder why people would like to live there. But when I saw its well-planned, tree-lined street, I was pleasantly surprised and, not for the first time, reminded myself not to make judgements on a place before I'd seen it.

As evening fell, I reached the outskirts of Whitehaven. Although the coal and iron trade which were the foundation of the town's prosperity have declined sharply in recent years, the town's Haig colliery, which runs under the sea, still supplies local blast furnaces, and the harbour still handles cargo. I locked my bike to a lamppost by the harbour and went into a local pub for a pie and a drop of what does you good.

I don't know whether it is true that the average age of the population is higher than elsewhere, but the people in the pub all seemed to be about seventy years old. The air was thick with pipesmoke as they sat in the corners with their Harris tweed caps on their heads. To a background of noise of clinking glasses and the crashing down of dominoes, everyone spoke the same. "Ey up, that's grand". One of the older men, a strong-looking man with a headful of blond hair, invited me to join them at their table. His name was Bill Grimshaw and he liked a pint or two.

"Me homebrew's not a bad drop of stuff", he said as he poked at the barrel of his pipe. I told him I got lost coming out of Barrow and we chatted about what I was doing. When he asked me what I did for a living, 'proper like', I told him I was an explorer and his pipe dropped out of his mouth. "An explorer", he cried in utter amazement, "that gets lost trying to get out of Barrer"! And the dominoes stopped chinking for a moment as rasping old men's chuckles came out from the corners of the room.

After he'd finished his third pint Bill asked me back to stay at his place for the night. "There's only the wife, but she'll feed you up". We walked about half a mile, me pushing my bike.

"Hello, luv", he said, giving his wife a kiss, "I've brought home an explorer who got lost in Barrer and he wants something to eat", and at this the chuckling old man sat down next to a big plastic container of homebrew. As his wife scurried into the kitchen, Mr Grimshaw sat upright, fiddled in his pocket for his pipe and said "Oscar Wilde was a glorified twentieth century pimp". He was full of unique little phrases was Mr Grimshaw. "A man cannot be honoured in his own time he has to be slaughtered first . . . look at Pericles". He obviously liked this one,

because over the next four pints he said it another three times.

"You and your Prickylees", said his wife, carrying in a tray of food. "It's the beer, dear", she muttered to me out of the corner of her mouth, "that's what does the talking", and she sat me down to a plate of egg and chips and a mug of steaming hot tea.

"Of course, you know what Mr Micawber said", he continued, "if you have 20 shillings and spend 19/6 that's good, but if you spend 20 shillings and 6d that will put you in penury". He paused, "my son, he spends all his money. He'll end up in clink and I won't be around to bale him out".

Mr Grimshaw had rather a thickset face, ruddy and kind. He never smiled, but when he laughed his pearly porcelain teeth clicked as his head shook up and down. "No, I'm not a philosopher. It's all a question of commonsense, a life that's been lived and three pints of best mild beer", and he slurped another half pint down for good measure.

Mr Grimshaw represented a generation of people who would smoke part of a cigarette, nipping it carefully with their fingers and replacing it in the box if it looked as though it might contain a few more puffs. He also epitomised a class of people who actually managed to celebrate ruby wedding anniversaries. He showed me bound volumes of the *Woodworkers' Weekly*, which took it for granted that wood for shelving was one hundred percent Canadian mahogany. He didn't only read 'the Woodworker', he was reading three other books at the time, Hammond Innes, Neville Shute and *The Easy Guide To Understanding V.A.T.* ("me son's got this funny business"). "I read poetry too", he said, "it's so transporting, isn't it? I look at Mermaid's pool and see a pool. A poet sees something quite different". I told him I thought everyone had some poetry in them, but he disagreed. "No, no, it's all to do with the genes and little brain cells and their juxtaposition with each other", and he filled his glass once more. "It unlocks the mind, you know". He wrapped his big old man's hands round his ankles and sat there, like a Buddha in a council house in Whitehaven.

The following morning, on my way to Carlisle, I had fond memories of Whitehaven and Mrs Grimshaw's egg and bacon fry. As the sparrows started to stir and rabbits dived out of the way of my silent wheels I remembered Mr Grimshaw's last wish to be young. "If I got to the pearly gates I'd say to God to put me under a banyan tree for five thousand years", he sat upright and sighed, "you know, to watch the pageant of life go by".

It was pleasant cycling on the road to Carlisle with the thoughts of 'Chairman Grimshaw' fresh as a daisy from a very old man tumbling around in my head. In Carlisle the milkman

B5302 to Carlisle 5.15 am.

Less than 10 miles out of Silloth and I don't feel very well. I feel nauseous and stop. Feeling very lightheaded. Can only think the reason may be because of the Chinese meal last night.

Sitting in a bus shelter on the side of the road I was sick. I had to sit down for half an hour until I felt less light headed. I anticipated bad patches but not so soon and that's a little worrying.

The Other Side of Dalbeattie

Lunch. 4 shredded wheat. (Ian Botham can only eat three!) Fried egg butties and steaming hot tea. I took a wrong turn and cut my rout's mileage by 8 miles. Ian's sticking his specs together with superglue as he comes out with his famous cliche 'Minutes Mean Miles'. Fly lands on the frying pan. "Here comes the meat dish", said Barry and some-one ate it.

Snack Bar on the Way to Newton Stewart

Quick ten minute stop at a tea stall. I feel quite good. The wind's dropped considerably making cycling just a bit easier. Kirkudbright seemed a very bright and airy town. Cycling around the coast the first time meant missing a lot of places. This time around it's almost impossible. My saddle's been giving me a few problems so Ian's swopping it with the spare bike. Barry's got a stomach upset "Cor I needed that", he said, "Must be three pounds lighter . . . "

Isle of Whithorn 7.10 pm.

Originally planned to reach Glenluce tonight but I think I'll settle for Port William. I thought anything after 200 miles would be a blur and I'd be knackered. It's a nice little harbour here, boats stand upright in the bay and a Cormorant croaks above. There's a pub at the end of the harbour and little boys play on their bikes outside. No-one else seems to live here and I can't think of any reason to be here apart from having to.

Silloth – Port William.

"O thou! Whatever title
suit thee, Auld Hornie,
Satan, Nick, or clootie"
Robbie Burns!

Mrs Katrina, all her life in farming and only once had a holiday

22

was still half asleep, the postman was shuffling about with his letters and even the sparrows were having a lie in today. Even Gretna, whose chief claim to fame is allowing runaway couples to marry without parental consent, was having a quiet first-thing-in-the-morning feeling.

On I peddled towards Dumfries, through the pale grey buildings of Dalbeattie and slightly inland to Kirkudbright, due to the main road being a couple of miles from the sea. I had only been to Scotland once before and that was only for a few days. I never thought of north of the border being a different country to England and how wrong I would be.

Two days after leaving England I arrived in a small place called Port William on the coast road to Stranraer. Barely a village, there was a small central square, a couple of telephone boxes, a bus shelter, three pubs and a cafe. A few houses were scattered about and apart from three plump adolescent girls there was no one around.

It was getting dark and the sea was getting grey. As I needed to camp I pushed my bike over to the small wall on which they were sitting and asked if they knew of a campsite. There was a pause, a look of bewilderment and a giggle. It was nice to hear some laughter, perhaps they would decide to help me.

"Dunno", said the third, "there's nothing much here," and immediately started giggling again.

"There's nae discos around here", said the first, "we ain't even got a town".

The highlight of their evening was an underage smoke on a shared cigarette as they watched each other's 'ex's' drive past in battered Cortinas.

They all looked alike with slightly inverted teeth and their legs were crammed into stone-washed jeans. One of the girls wore a badge saying 'I like the simple things in life – men' and another had one saying 'Get stoned – drink wet cement'.

At nine in the evening the only place to get a meal and a cup of tea was a cafe full of space invaders and pinball machines and air stale with the smell of a thousand cigarettes. In the corner of a small room I sat by a pool table next to a window overlooking the harbour and ordered a plate of chips and a cup of tea.

"All the girls are buzzin' now ye're in town", said the cafe proprietoress looking at me just a fraction longer than was comfortable. I muttered something which included the word 'ridiculous' and she stopped pouring my tea to talk. "Well ye're famous, aren't you"? she demanded rhetorically, "all people who live in London are, aren't they"?

"I don't live in London and I'm not famous," I began, glancing down at my chips which were beginning to go cold.

"Ye're new though, aren't you"? she persisted, determined that even if I were not a notable eccentric I was at least recognisably a foreigner from the south and therefore to be gossiped about and bandied around for days after I'd gone. It was easy for me to be an exotic bird of

passage in Port William where a trip to London was a journey to the moon and Northern France at the boundaries of space and time.

To say Port William was dull was a compliment, I dare say on a rainy day it was worse, and I couldn't think of any reason why people continued to live here apart from economic reasons long since dried up.

Next morning I woke up to a bracing sea air and a steady drizzle of rain. If I missed the Mull of Galloway it would be twenty three and a half miles to Stranrear and by the time I had got there the drizzle had stopped.

Towns in Scotland were smaller than I had imagined. From a distance, Stranraer was just a name, giving no indication that it was anything other than a port and had a football team. At half past six in the morning it was sleepy and I cycled quietly down Hanover Street to the tinkling of Radio One. A cormorant shrieked over the wide, sweeping bay and fishermen poked around for a lugworm breakfast for their catch. The day was still overcast and underneath a concrete bus shelter daubed with 'The Eurythmics are cool', I took a quick nap.

The wind was behind me and the road north to Ayr was reasonably flat and where the Water of Girvan swings through a final meandering curve to empty into the Firth of Clyde I entered Girvan.

Over the next few days I peddled on to Ayr, past the golf club at Troon, the new town at Irvine and eventually Gourock.

The lighthouse at Gourock was beautiful. Painted white with a black trim, the walls and tower were thick and solid. Lighthouses are not so much built as chiseled out of the ground. Standing alone as the evening sky turned from the pallor of pale blue to a more robust turquoise, I watched the beam of the lighthouse sweep across the Firth of Clyde to Dunoon.

The street on both sides of the Firth glistened and shone in the last remnants of a rainy sun. A sunbeam spot-lit a single yacht to the sound of a barking dog and the gentle tired whoosh of tiny waves on the shore.

The vaster, wilder tracts of Scotland had to be approached differently from the more heavily populated England. Hours would pass before I'd reach a shop or a pub and if I was given an occasional nod I would regard myself pleased with conversation for the day. This part of Scotland seemed full of smooth flat roads hugging the sides of lochs which were as still as a mirror. Wherever the hills closed in to form a valley I wanted to shout across the water and echo to the distant shore. I found people here conservative and forthright, friendly and welcoming, not in the slightest bit suspicious of me trespassing from the south. Already I felt I was in a different country, but I was to be surprised at the extent of this difference as I carried on further north.

Port William – Gourock.

Outskirts of Stranraer 7.30 a.m.

Had quite a good night's sleep but woke up with a heavy head cold. I find it very hard to get up early and 5.00 a.m. is early. The wind is pushing me along and progress has been very good and I sit on a bench again overlooking the bay. Eating peanuts, a group of gulls hover nearby. I throw a few but only one brave fellow dares retrieve his prize while the rest just laugh and chortle to slowly drift away.

Inbetween Ary and Troon 12.15 p.m.

Stopped for lunch in a small road off the coastal road to Troon. Having covered 100 miles I'm ahead of schedule. Lost the back-up car all morning because of the tailwind. They had difficulty catching me up. The lads are cooking eggs and bacon and I'm resting in the car. Even though the wind was behind me it started to rain at about 6.30 a.m. and fell very heavily all morning. Climbed Cow Brae, and electric hill. I was definately going uphill and felt as if I was freewheeling downhill, very strange.

The Nethermains Junction on the A78 towards Greenock

I'd just made a phone call on the outskirts of Irvine New Town. The back-up car had missed me and it was raining. The dual carriageway was quiet as I approached a road from the left. A yellow British Rail van slowly drove up, I thought he would stop. As I crossed his path I could see from the corner of my eye he wasn't stopping, I accelerated fractionally and he hit my back wheel. The next thing I knew I was sprawled out in the middle of the road. I stood up immediately and told him he was responsible and he said he never even saw me.

Largs 7.10 p.m.

My legs have cramped up and I'm finding it hard to cycle. The accident has put me so far behind schedule. I really must go on. The wind if anything has got stronger and it's turned into a cross wind blowing me all over the place.

Gourock 9.30 p.m.

Knocked on some-one's door and she kindly let us use her caravan and a nice warm bath. Fish and chips and brown bread and butter for tea. Barry doesn't feel too well. He's virtually overdosed on peanuts. Ian gives us a rendition of the latest words he's learning: 'pendantry' and 'somnambulist'. Barry said, "Crapulence... is the effect of too much partying" . . . Humour is vital in such a tightly scheduled working day, and being 80 miles down on schedule is really quite worrying.

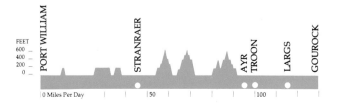

FEET
600
400
200
0

0 Miles Per Day   50   100

PORT WILLIAM   STRANRAER   AYR   TROON   LARGS   GOUROCK

Day 4

Gourock – Lochgilphead.

Helensburg 8.15 a.m.
After yesterday's crash I've taken the first 40 miles fairly easily. It was raining with a slight headwind and my legs were very tense. With the wind and the heavy lidded overcast sky it's bound to rain. As I cycle through Helensburg the team car arrives and Ian comments that the town is as interesting as cold toast for breakfast which was a little unfair as I quite liked it.

On the Road to Arrachur 9.50 a.m.
Bacon and egg plus four more shredded wheat. Breakfast is something I really look forward to. Mealtimes are about the only time I talk to anyone. Over the glen a hooter blows, it's either a tea-break or they're shining their new cruise missiles.

South of Ardentinny 12.00p.m.
85 miles covered. About 135 miles to go. I'm falling behind schedule all the time which is intentional. I need to get through this first week as comfortably as possible particularly as the hills are fairly steep and it's always raining. Still apart from the hills, the rain, the cold and the long miles, the early starts, the late finishing and the midges, there are compensations. The lakes are very beautiful, especially in a mist. The roads are extremely quiet.

Clachaig 1.45 p.m.
Stopped for lunch, had to phone home. A couple of old Scots passed by and read the side of the car as Barry was asking directions. '22 Days, a new world record, and ya don't know where ya goin', that's a good record son . . . !

Near Strachur 6.30 p.m.
Such a beautiful Loch, such wonderful winding single track roads. When the sun shines the daffodils stand out against soft green fields. I'm going very well indeed so have managed to snatch five minutes. A cup of tea, a packet of peanuts and Frank Muir on Radio 4.

Lochgilphead 9.15 p.m.
After cycling about 210 miles I feel quite pleased. Don't feel in the slighest bit shattered. After 150 miles I felt as if I was in a steady state phase. I was hardly breathing. If only I could see more of beautiful Scotland, the scenery is absoloutely breathtaking. Fish and chips again for tea in the tent. 210 miles plus a day around Scotland on Shredded Wheat, bacon butties and fish and chips . . . great! The milage I'm, losing here will have to be made up in England. Comfortable beds and steak will possibly help.

'Rest and be thankful' said the sign, and I was!

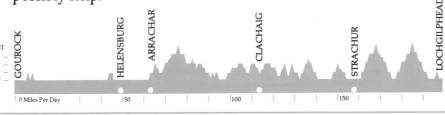

TIGH NA TRAIGH

TIGHNABRUAICH
4 MILES

*Top Left, boats at rest
around Ullapool harbour*

On the Way to Campbeltown 6.30 a.m.
Stopped to take my waterproof jacket off. It's stopped raining and the sun's shining. Feeling stiff from yesterday in the hills. Should be easier by Saturday. In the valley a herring gull calls creating an echo as he flies to and fro for food. The clouds move very fast, a mixture of black cloud and blue sky.

Tayinloan 9.00 a.m.
Giving the back up crew an extra hour in bed it takes a while for them to catch me up. As I took a wrong turn off the main road in Tarbert I saw them drive past without seeing me. Expect we'll meet up in Campbeltown. Such a dreary, overcast day. Scotland is beautiful apart from the weather and the midges. Bought some chocolate at Tayinloan stores, a couple of ladies serve everything from rubber bands to cans of beans. School children line up until the bus turns up. People come and go and to all intents and purposes life goes on very well even though geographically everything is so distant here.

Campbeltown 10.45 a.m.
Coming to places like Cambeltown makes you realise how widely scattered Scotland is. The cycling to get here is long and hard. After yesterday I now feel very stiff. There's no doubt I'm finding it difficult to concentrate. Some days will be good, some bad. So far it's overcast and dull and I've 70 miles yet to do.

The Peninsula of West Loch Tarbert
Single track road for 32 miles. Felt very relaxed, ambling along at 15mph. A very strange grass cutter stopped me for a chat, telling me that he'd met the fellow who last biked around the coast. He did 50 miles a day, far more dignified. Further along I met a man cycling with his pet dog, Sandy, sitting in a box on the carrier. And for a moment I lay down to remember what it was like to fall asleep in the sun.

Field on The Outskirts of Cornell 9.30 p.m.
It's been a hard day again. Rarely a flat section, always the hills. After such a miserable start to the day, the sun shone warmly and everybody's spirits raised. Unfortunately days at the moment are long and tired a bit drawn out. Team morale is low, tired perhaps and I must sort out the problem. After 200 miles a day in very hard terrain it's not easy to appreciate other people's problems. I'm sure by tomorrow everyone will be more tolerant.

Lochgilphead – Cornell.

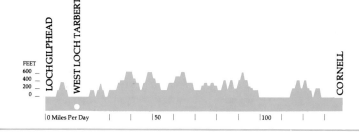

Cycling on to the outskirts of town I put up my tent near the bridge at Connel. Thank goodness for the likes of Hamish Oberoy Junior, it gives life a proper perspective again.

Ideally, I wanted to cycle further north to Mallaig, the Kyle of Lochalsh, Ullapol and Durness. Knowing I was going that way later in the year within '22 Days' I decided to cross country along Loch Ness to that compact, charming little town, Inverness.

Being so far north meant I was surrounded and infused with hard core Scottish culture. A note for tourists from Murray's Handbook for Scotland 1894 always made me smile. "The Scottish middle and lower classes are not, as a rule, given to joking, except with their own dry sententious humour, and they very rarely understand what is commonly called 'chaff'. It is better to bear this in mind, as it may account for many an apparently surly manner or gruff reply".

Known as the 'capital town of the Highlands', Inverness is situated on the River Ness with seven bridges across its waters. The seventh bridge was completed in 1939, which coincided with the outbreak of the Second World War. As local legend would have it, some people saw this as a fulfillment of a prophecy made by a soothsayer known as the Brahan Seer about three centuries before. He prophesied that when there were seven bridges across the River Ness, the women of the town would weep for their dead. The capture of the 51st Inverness Division who fought the rearguard action at Dunkirk in 1940 seemed to fulfill the ancient sage's warning.

For much of the time in Scotland I slept outside in a small one-man tent. A major problem at dusk are the midges which hunt in packs, descending on naked flesh like flying piranhas that haven't been fed for a week. Mr Murray in his famous guidebook takes this into account when giving advice to tourists and cyclists alike. "The traveller in the west of Scotland,

Sealochs and swans and bright white-washed churches

among the lochs and rivers, is subjected to an intolerable insect plague of midges – small gnats, scarcely visible, but covering the face with painful and enduring punctures. Prince Charlie, in his year of hiding, 1746, was nearly driven distracted by them. Ammonia is very efficacious in removing the pain of the stings; and tobacco smoke, or a little paraffin oil rubbed on any exposed part of the skin is a good preventative of the attacks of these assailants. Turpentine is said to be an antidote, but the cure is almost as bad as the disease".

By evening I had passed through Nairn and Elgin, Buckie, and Macduff until after a hundred miles of lovely rolling plains I saw the granite dustbin of Fraserburgh.

Fraserburgh was one of those sea-shore burghs which come into being at the initiative of a landowner. Sir Alexander Fraser, 7th Laird of Pillorth, obtained a charter in 1546 'to build a harbour in which ships overtaken by storms may find refuge'. Instead he left a terraced mountain of municipal granite, stone faced and suspicious with the look of a convict on the run.

In the long granite streets the houses stood bleakly, plain and unadorned. There were no front gardens because costcutting Sir Alexander had created an efficient working town which didn't deserve good people to live in it. If only the residents could leave it behind every night and just commute in to work there I'm sure the air would not hang so heavy. Fish processing plants leaked all over town and sullen working girls smelled of cheap perfume and whitebait. Dirty-nosed little boys hung on to the odd picked-up fish head and little girls pointed at me and laughed. Young mothers pushing prams watched me cautiously, ready to cross to the other side of the road if I made a sudden move. My first impression of Fraserburgh was that the best that could be said for it was that it would be even worse on a windy day, and I left.

Day 6

Cornell – Cuaig.

Slightly South of Fort William 9.15 a.m.

Covered 45 miles this morning, feeling OK. The lack of wind turned Loch Creran into a mirror. I shouted to hear an echo but it was very faint. Breakfast is as ever four shredded wheat except that this morning Barry, in his capacity as chief chef has fried me four sausages and a piece of last night's steak. It's still overcast and I'm already counting the days when I can leave the West Coast of Scotland. Rain is imminent and the midges are everywhere. Must reach Kyle of Localsh by 1.15 p.m.

Invergarry Phone Box 11.00 a.m.

Just passed through quite a famous statue surrounded by tourists. Funny looking up at them looking down at me from their tourist buses chomping away on their packed lunches.

Localsh Hotel 3 p.m.

Just finished a 2 hour broadcast with Piccadilly Radio as the Isle of Skye ferry plies to and fro. And the wind is warm and I've another 100 miles to go. It's so tranquil here, you really want to stay. In a way you wonder why I cycle 220 miles a day when you could sit on the quayside watching the ferry just sail on by.

On the Banks of Loch Carron

A boat sits solitarily in the loch far down the hillside. The odd car passes and the wind is very still. In the distance I hear seagulls and I'm quite a way off my schedule.

Cuaig 8.30 pm

Applecross. Along Loch Kishorn to Cuaig, a village with one house. I'm very tired tonight and can hardly write. Barry and Ian chat and wash in the stream near the tents. I feel a bit isolated because I'm still full of apprehension for each days mileage. Each day I lose a few more miles and wonder if I'll catch up in the flatter area like Norfolk. This is certainly the hardest stretch of the journey I shall have. Just hope I don't lose too much time. Dinner tonight was tomato soup, canned potatoes and pears followed by canned beef burgers with onions and gravy. Bed and Breakfast will seem such a luxury. "We'll have to go to a hotel soon", said our chief driver. "We're running out of bog paper".

Another Scottish loch that seems to go on forever.

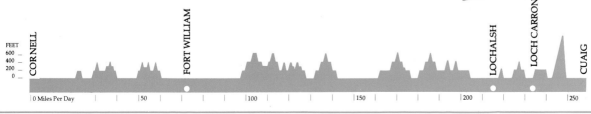

Top Left, facing page, Scourie

35

When to the sessions of sweet silent thought
I summon up rememberance of things past
I sigh the lack of many a thing I sought
And with old woes new wail my dear times waste:

Tea was served out of her best silver teapot and the family cow provided rich creamy milk. The table was set for breakfast. Bone handled cutlery given to Mrs Mackay from her mother. The tablecloth was embroidered cotton, fresh and spotless.

Fellow cyclists on their travels round Scotland and one with a trailer on the look-out for work

Home Made Butter and Creamy Jersey Milk

Up at 5.00 a.m. Mrs. Mackay made me eggs and bacon washed down with a steaming pot of tea, oatmeal bread, milk from her own jersey cow. I told her how different I thought Scotland was compared to England. She said it was because there weren't any 'darkies' here. "Well, we do have a Pakistani shop in town, but I don't patronise him". And then as she hand churned her butter and hand milked her cow, this is the highlands of Scotland, untouched and pure where Geordies, Englishmen and Pakis all fear to tread.

Mrs Mackays B & B – Boghead of Orrack.

Blue stocking Girls in Inverness 11.30 a.m.

So all the girls in Inverness wear blue stockings. Well I wonder if they are blue stocking women! Covered 140 miles since 5.00 a.m., around Cromarty, the Black Isle and to Inverness. A lovely town. After coming down from the Highlands anywhere is busy. It's nice to see people shop and watch old men curse at bus drivers and people with heir all shades of pink and blue. In a busy town like this I feel less of a foreigner. Being in a city gives you a certain anonymity in which to hide in, something the villages never do.

I feel quite good knowing I've only got 100 miles yet to go. And as another blue stocking girl in Inverness walked past me, she gives my bare knees a passing glance.

The Wooden Spoon Cafe at Nairn 2.00 p.m.

After Inverness I've got a strong tail wind blowing me along and I don't feel tired at all. It must be Mrs Mackays hand churned butter. A quick egg on toast in the cafe and back on the road.

The Road to Fraserburg

80 miles from Inverness on the coast road. A tailwind. Fraserburg was like a prison. Grey granite houses that lead out onto the street. Loose people walk around, a disproportionate share of girls made up to high heaven and really nowhere to go. As I sat on the pavement watching the people going by I realised I'd biked 210 miles so far on eggs and bacon, one egg on toast and half a bottle of Vimto. A fair was in town, a feat in itself reaching this far east. And the town reeked of a fish canning factory and as I left for the last 20 miles, the air was full of hair spray.

Boghead of Orrack 11.30 p.m.

Unable to find B & B we ended up in the field of a local farmer. Boghead was the name of the farm, Orrack the name of the village. Mr. Boghead's wife brought out 2 pints of milk and a trifle and Mr. Boghead gave me a flask of hot water. It's light enough to read at 11.30 p.m., and I'm shattered.

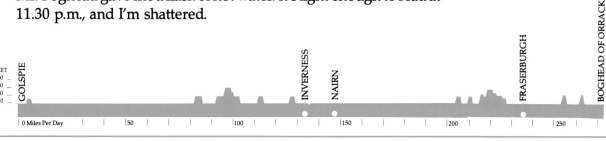

Across the meadow, Bamburgh Castle

The lady and the tramp; Edinburgh

dictated
fickleness
rampage

As th
big fat Si
chips ar
can with
stands u
slung be
face loo
seagulls
Yorkshir
sky blue

As ha
pared to
ten-mile
road, I a
looking
today ha
that out
to see. T
timistic f
cepting a
travelling
cept an
rosemar
against a
good jou
maximis
place. It
derstand
the very
travelling
tand ze
speaking
that the s
instead
robbery
on the
delights
possibly

Medical Centre
Stretcher Cases
Only

51

Waiting at the traffic lights in Great Yarmouth I was wondering whether to follow the 'AA' sign that read 'Faith Healing' when I heard a voice calling me. "Hello, I saw you at the Norfolk restaurant; come and have a chat".

We sat down on a bench watching the traffic go by. I could tell he wanted a little company and the price of a cup of tea.

"I used to work the Thames barges see". And his face screwed up into a thousand lines.

"What now. I get £33 a week and me digs cost me £30. Me on me pension and the youngsters get twice that on the dole. They say, "grandad lend us some sugar" and I tell 'em to "buggar off and stop wastin' it all in the pub".

Like all sailors' faces, his was firm and kind. The sea seems to give her passengers a pride and respect, an understanding of a force far greater than oneself. The sea also takes away teeth and puckers chins, breaking blood vessels in healthy cheeks and they go red and the whites of the eyes are near blue as they sag like the great greedy black-backed belly slung around squawking face, squinting into the wind.

These were my thoughts as it was breezy on the beach watching the traffic go by. Mr Reginald wasn't tatty or unkempt but I knew he hadn't got very much.

"Ere go and see a mate o' mine at Malden,

you said you ain't got a proper job", And he scribbled an address on a piece of paper he'd fished out of his pocket.

"Give you a job 'ee will, sailing barges for the summer. Ask for Mad Mike Polly and old Tubby Blake at the Jolly Sailor, they'll know me".

At that Mr Reginald stood up and we shook hands as he asked for the price of a cup of tea. Gladly.

It wasn't far to Lowestoft and immediately one felt the close impact Great Yarmouth had on the town. As an entertainment centre Lowestoft required much but was a nice place to be with a beautiful frontage it made up for the lack of computerised opiates.

Tall bay windowed town houses grace the front, towering over the prom looking out to Dogger Bank. White wrought iron railings clasp the finely chiseled masonry and a glance through the gleaming windows reveals a

musty conversation. Silver plated cutlery rest on quite white tablecloths in teashops called 'Buttries'. Along the wide promenade hatpinned old ladies walk arm in arm and husbands dawdle behind talking cricket.

Before long I was in Ipswich, winding my way through rumbling rush hour traffic until I came to a green bench near the centre of town. Henry V111th once said of Ipswich that the women here were amongst the most beautiful in the land and I would only but humbly agree.

As in Edinburgh there is something sedate in the way the girls stroll along. Idly shopping without a care at all, the beautiful people of the world, popping in the shop for a red fox fur.

Colchester too was a very pleasant town. The long rising high street leading up to the town hall and the gentle parade of shops either side. I should like to have spent more time in Colchester, one of the oldest towns in Britain but I had to press on to London.

A morning later I was cycling along red paving stones which gave the High Street in Rochester an impression of antiquity. Purveyors of fine Tea and Coffee scented the street with all manner of exotic aromas – black coffee beans roasted underneath a Kenyan sun, tea from Darjeeling smelling of muscatel grapes, Chinese orange pekoe and, as ever my favourite, the balmy lemon tang of Earl Grey.

Rochester was certainly a town full of grace and charm. Watercolour art galleries sold quality silk hangings, Japanese prints by Hokusai and the odd Lowry, just a little incongruously placed. Charles Dickens called Rochester Dullborough, a trifle unfair perhaps, particularly as Mr Jingle explored the castle whilst Mr Pickwick resided at the Royal Victoria and Bull Hotel.

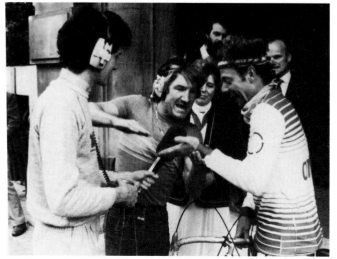

Piccadilly Radio at Colchester

Day 14

Brixton Hill – Eastbourne.

Westminster Abbey 6.10 a.m.

The sun's shining now the wind's dropped. We're on the bridge. Ian's setting up his cameras and Barry sets up the bikes. I'm off to meet Frank Dickens the cartoonist at St. Paul's cathedral at 6.30 a.m. and Ian says he's ready to take a photo of me cycling across the bridge.

6.35 a.m. Frank Dickens and Mr Bristow

I really enjoyed cycling with Frank, this was the first and only occasion I had enjoyed cycling company. He seemed to enjoy the day into Kent and he was very knowledgeable about cycling. He gave me a signed copy of his new book 'Three Cheers For The Good Guy'. The star is a racing cyclist called Dicks. I wonder if it's secretly autobiographical and that he's a frustrated racing cyclist like me.

The Queens Hotel Eastbourne

After having to ride into the wind all afternoon I passed through the flat plains of Romney Marsh. Arriving once again in Eastbourne was somewhat more auspicous this time than the last. The Mayor welcomed me at the best hotel in town. From my room I can see the Pier and the sea crashes onto the shore. Such are the extremes of this journey that one moment I'm sleeping in a field full of cows, the next a four star hotel. Presently I am very very tired indeed. Too tired to brush my teeth, too tired to focus. My vision goes out of focus and it takes all my effort to look at this page. Sometimes I wonder if the journey will end and the next minute wonder if I'll miss it once its finished. The waves crash on the pebbles and a few girls laugh and chatter in the street below. Cars pass by the light of the pier and I undress and sleep.

It was quite hilly cycling up to East Dean, over the beautiful cliff chalklands, and out of the mist down to the Seven Sisters country park, where the river was meandering into oxbow lakes. Down into Seaford, then egg, fried bread, beans, sausage and tea for £1.

One place I was really looking forward to visiting was Brighton – the queen of seaside resorts. Here the virtues of sea water were first publicised and promoted on a large scale. Its 19th Century hotels, the Metropole and the Grand, were the forerunners of seaside palaces that stretched from the Riviera to Florida, Acapulco to the Seychelles. And in the Royal Pavillion, commissioned by George III's flamboyant eldest son, hangs a painting by Whistler. Called 'The Prince Regent Awakening the Spirit of Brighton', it shows the almost naked prince lifting the veil from a sleeping girl. If Blackpool was brash and Mablethorpe dull, Great Yarmouth ordinary and Eastbourne sedate, Brighton was raffish bohemia itself.

Freewheeling past a grocer's shop in Kemptown, I noticed that between the shredded wheat and the tins of pineapple chunks there were people seated, drinking tea. Two girls were chatting by the bananas and next to a shelf stuffed with bags of rice sat a solemn looking man. One of the girls got up to serve me a cup of Darjeeling costing 30p. Such is the trendy affectation that dictates you sip expensive tea as someone reaches over your table to purchase half a pound of Camembert and a glass of Burgundy.

The other girl meanwhile read out a clue from the Daily Telegraph crossword: "a standard type of paving stone … four down". Just as tea is 'mashed' and sandwiches turn into 'butties', north of England paving stones become 'flags'. The first time I'd ever got a clue right!

"Someone's had a good night's sleep", said the solemn man in the corner who looked like Oswald Moseley. I told him I'd spent the previous night in a field.

"Ploughed fields are the best", he said, flattening down his pencil moustache with his moistened forefinger. Mr Moseley had a slim face with hollow cheeks, his dark glasses shielded convex eyes from view. He sat nervously, legs crossed and hands clasped around a cup and saucer.

"I once spent a night in an egg box by Hong Kong harbour", I said.

"Ah", he replied, "one night in an egg box and you're not the same again". There must have been something in what he said, but I wasn't quite sure of what.

"Of course, you do know the correct way that one should sleep in an egg box, don't you"? He was determined to tell me, whether I wanted to know or not. I reckoned on an upright position, if it were a dry night, the open top facing up.

"Wind dynamics, my dear boy, wind dynamics . . . an egg box must always lie on its side". I slurped a little more Darjeeling and Mr Moseley looked very serious. "The wind goes around the earth hugging the surface and when it comes to the open top of an egg box it hugs that too, dipping into it. Put it on its side, put it on its side". And with an exasperated sigh at the extent of my ignorance of aerodynamics he got up and left.

Ever since Henry VIII holidayed adulterously here, this part of the south coast has had a healthy disregard for the establishment. After her second visit Queen Victoria refused to come again, sniffing air that was less than sacrosanct.

How lovely Brighton must have been just over a hundred years ago; with the bathing machines, the Brighton Belles that never got wet, Punch and Judy and saucy postcards which started a vogue for the caption with a double meaning.

Leaving it was a wrench, for despite its eccentrics and air of gay abandon, my feelings would be impaired for towns further along the coast. Within an hour I'd passed Hove, Portslade, Shoreham-by-Sea and Worthing and was on the verge of leaving Littlehampton when I saw a cafe to my liking. Any cafe opposite a railway station tends to be downtrodden and seedy, an inbetween place briefly frequented by people on the move. Squashed into something less than the size of a living room were ten tables, forty-two chairs, a Space Invader, slot machine, half a dozen variously assorted youths and a small cross-eyed, balding proprietor who stood menacingly behind his 'kitchen'.

"Ah what you want, ze tea or ze carfee? I make no good ze tea but eet is cheap . . ."

As his eyes wern't looking at me I looked around to see who he was talking to.

" 'ello you. I talk to you, I make ze tea".

"Italian or Greek"? I said.

"Cessena", he said, "you know, ze abbey, ze walls", and on his paper-wood walls hung pictures of St. Peter's Square and Florence. We chatted as he passed the tea and my journeying seemed to please him. He had married a girl from Oldham and he wouldn't let me pay for my drink. Sitting down I noticed several boys and girls staring at me as if I'd stepped off the moon that afternoon. A tall boy was gambling hard at the slot machine. At present rates of exchange his social security payments gave him 270 goes a week. Next to him an insipid-looking girl hung around for nothing. She hadn't anywhere to go and not a lot to do apart from pierce her own ears to make her head drop lopsided.

The proprietor's name was Frank. He came over with a bag of haddock and chips and another mug of tea, saying "No pay, no pay". It was hard to believe that the first free meal I'd been given on my journey was from little fat Frank from Cessena.

Towns on the south coast, like Littlehampton and Middleton, Worthing and Bognor, have all fused together in one stodgy, little heap. Togetherness is sameness in this long ribbon of predictable surburbia united in spirit by people who live in bungalows and clean their cars on a Sunday afternoon.

On this part of the coast it's easier to notice similiarities than peculiarities. The town centre is a precinct with Wimpys, Woolworths and 'Coffee Cup' cafes and faceless people who drive around in second hand Ford Fiestas. The girls walk around on matchstick-thin legs without a smile or a glance or a wave. And the boys chase the girls and the girls play hard to get in that precinct, somewhere on a dreary afternoon.

The Romans called Chichester Noviomagus, and the town centre still has the simple logic of its Roman plan: four main streets, north, south, east and west meeting at a central point and surrounded by a circular wall. Standing, chatting to an old cyclist on his bike I told him where I'd come from.

"I weep when I go to Manchester, all the derelict buildings, the filled-in canals, falling down back-to-back houses . . . " When he spoke, his stubby fingers scratched his white, crew-cropped head tentatively. "You see, the problem lies with infant mortality which used to be ten percent but is now less than one percent. Medicine, hygiene better food . . ." The point he was trying to make was that by increasing infant mortality it gives the rest of us a chance. "And you know what that means – breeding. People breed you know, in a line, an exponential curve and before you know where you are everywhere will look like Manchester", he said, balancing on his bright red worn out knee caps.

How the old can sneer about the world the young have to make do with! It's always the violence, the tarts, the wicked workers of iniquity and the beating up of old ladies. It's always 'the dirty greasy yobs' or 'the weird looking punks' and the skinheads with trails of pale white scar tissue.

A day or so later I was in Southampton, cycling along wide Upper Bar Gate. *The Mikado* was playing that night and on the posters a few lines aptly summed up the life of a port.

'The happiest hour a sailor sees
Is when he's down
At an inland town
With his Nancy on his knees, yo ho! yo ho!
And his arm around her waiste!

As ships are few and press gangs no longer roam the streets, I thought I'd try Bournemouth for an afternoon's excitement.

Day 16

Lyme Regis – Penzance.

Lyme Regis

The latest start on the trip, 7.20 a.m. I just didn't want to go. Today will be hard and yesterday was very hard towards the end. I anticipate two days of grind and then it should be a little easier by Wednesday. South Wales will be easy compared to this.

Feel absolutely wretched. Cycled to Exeter and on the outskirts of town found a grass bank and lay down. It's a beautiful English summer day and I don't want to go on. I get up and hear the traffic and want to hide away. The journey is now taking its toll. 220 miles a day in the hills, in the rain, in the wind has taken away enthusiasm.

Plymouth 2.30 p.m.

At last the support car has caught up with me. For large sections of the day I'm on my own whilst Ian's taking photographs at his own pace. In the meantime I suffer and grumble but it really is the only way it can be done. Lunch is four shredded wheat, a peanut butter sandwich and about four pints of Vimto. The temperature is low eighties, a nice temperature for cycling, lovely when the wind blows. Feeling a bit better mentally, but am ever so tired. Want to fall asleep right now.

On the Way to Truro

Coming to a dead stop up the hills. It's not that my legs haven't the strength but that I need sleep. I nearly nodded off cycling up one of the hills and had to rest for ten minutes. I had to be woken up to continue. It all seems absurd at the moment but I know I'll hang on now 'til the end. It would be such a waste if I didn't.

B & B in Penzance 10.00 p.m.

What a day! It's been so hard. At one stage I didn't think I'd be able to carry on possibly the first and only day I felt like this. It's so nice sitting in the bath knowing there's a hot meal waiting and a comfy bed. The seagulls were very welcoming surely the noisiest I ever heard.

Zzzzzz...! Nearly nodded off while still on my bike ... Phew!

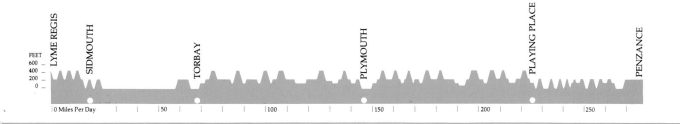

Dreaming alone on the edge of Britain.

The first thing I noticed about Bournemouth was how bright the light was. Looking out to sea by the Pier Theatre I was squinting into white sea fog. Sitting on the prom I watched two boys cycle down a short flight of stairs to the pebble-scattered beach over and over again. One was short and curly-haired, the other flushed and chubby with a fishing rod strapped to his bike. Under the pier it seemed very like Blackpool and two lovers kissed. "There's more to life than snogging, Barry", the girl said heavily overcoated against a cold breeze as they carried on with blue fingers. Upright lamp standards, gunmetal grey, lined the shore as an old man in an astrakhan hat struggled to read his flapping *Evening Echo*.

Opposite the tourist bureau 'Dingles' restaurant is near to 'Dingles Holidays', which is next to 'Dingles House of Fraser' selling small square Chinese rugs for only £600. Around the corner on Richmond Hill, Foxy's tea shop sells pots of tea for 35p. As I sat sipping gently, con-

templating the brown checked table cloths, I reckoned this the cheapest tea in the country! With its impressive redbrick frontage, even the police station is refined in Bournemouth, and with that I left for Lyme Regis.

It was evening in Lyme Regis and the steep, narrow main street leading to the harbour was bathed in quiet lamp light. There was hardly any wind and no noise save for the occasional "goodnight" and the sea slipping gently between pebbles in the bay. In the 1880's Lyme Regis Borough Council issued stern edicts against lecherous males who rowed anywhere near the wheeled bathing machines from which young ladies shyly dipped. Etiquette prevails in Lyme Regis above all else and as the occasional strand of bunting waved, young men accompanied young ladies without having yet reached the balmy thrill of holding hands. The town cryer walked up to the Volunteer pub in his navy blue and red tunic, it had been a hard day's crying.

Day 17

Lands End 7.30 a.m.

Pedalled the last ten minutes to Lands End in warm sunshine. For a moment I was in Brittany cycling to the boulangerie for my bagette and croissants. Anything has to feel better than yesterday.

A pale green fishing smack drifts by the rocks below. Seagulls cry and scavenge and even on a calm day the waves pound heavily on the End itself. Lands End is certainly more dramatic than John O' Groats and if I ever do an end to end event I'd prefer to finish here.

Land marks like this do make a coastal journey that much easier. People have asked me if the journey is easier than cycling around the world or the Journey to the Source of the Nile. In one sense it is, good food and accommodation in the only country I know something about. But the isolation is there all the same. The long hours on the bike, the terrible fatigue and an intense desire to achieve something, but I'm not sure what. And sitting here listening to the gulls and the waves in the wind and the sun I know these 22 days are not the most important part of the project and never were.

On the road to Portreath

Extreme lethargy has finally set in. The one thing that could thwart the journey is lack of sleep. Without sleep the incentive is blurred and I can't always work out why or what I'm doing. I look up at the blue sky and wish I were a cloud or a wisp of wind over the sea; clouds and wind seem to have it so easy. My eyes go out of focus as I write and I feel dizzy. I close one eye and as if wakening from a falling dream, jerk forward. My eyes just will not focus near to unless I consciously make them.

Penzance – Clovelly.

CHEERS!

Just a stone's throw away I freewheeled down the mainstreet of Beer to the beach. Jack Rattenbury, one of Devon's most celebrated smugglers, was a native here. Smuggling swagbags of contraband under a moonlit Devon night has such a romantic appeal you almost feel like applying for the job. Fishing boats with green hulls are called Tweedledum and Tweedledee and orange and green nets sprawl in the sun to dry. A large gannet leaps out from the cliff to catch the occasional morsel as deck chairs are stacked end to end ever hopeful for the season to start.

Just after Beer, on the road to Sidmouth, I stopped to talk to a lovely old man who had nothing better to do than lean against a country gate and watch the world go by. He reckoned that people were like ants scurrying about making ridiculous things seem quite important.

"Why go to the moon when all we need is this"? he exclaimed pointing to the hedgerow he stood next to. "Bluebells, known as wild hyacinth in Scotland, hairless, bulbous perenial". There were lots of bluebells and a few snapdragons and rosebay willow herb, frilly and pink. "Did you know, hyacinth commemorates a Greek youth mourned by Appollo the sun-god when he was killed by a discus thrown by the jealous Zephyrus, god of the west wind"? I told him I thought it was just a rumour and that bluebells were really used to hang around the necks of naked nymphs to dance in a circle in the forest. It was nice to see him laugh, it made his eyes sparkle.

It was a pleasure to stop and talk to this man by his five-barred gate. He was very schoolteacherish; short-cropped hair, half-moon glasses, a kind, square face on top of a rumpled tweed jacket. Ex-army, ex-grammar, the name was Herbert Ivan Brown, born 1898. He spent a lot of time dreaming wistfully in the summery sun. His wife had died eight years ago and 'the pain never goes away'.

"You're a writer", he said, "may I read you a poem about my wife? It's called 'The Kingfisher'". I told him I'd be delighted and he cleared his throat and carefully straightened his tie.

Bluebird of Happiness and truest love.
Dear flashing jewel of secret stream
In existing tenderness.
The gleam of wings of paradise
Exalts above the realm of space and time
My ravished heart.
You are the essence of most dear delight.

The only appreciation of poetry I have is whether I like it or not, and I told him it was wonderful. A tear crept into his eye and as he shook my hand he said I'd made his day by listening to him, but really it was the other way round. I climbed on to my bike and headed for Exeter.

There was nothing really brash about this part of the coast and not a lot that was exciting. I wasn't bored but life hadn't got the murky grit that I was used to picking out of my teeth. People were friendly enough but that was the sum total of it – people are friendly to strangers passing by, just enough to keep them moving, not enough to make them stay. I felt an intruder in Exeter. No doubt a loveable city for some, with Mols Coffee House and Sir Francis Drake's favourite tavern, the Ship Inn. The cathedral is remarkable; Exeter Maritime Museum the world's largest collection of boats, but not much use to a stranger on his own.

In a country as small as Britain it seems ridiculous to suggest that anywhere is far away. But for the first time on my journey I felt far away from home. It had taken me weeks to get here and it would take me weeks to get back. Sitting on the wall of Cathedral Close by St. Peters an old lady was feeding the birds. Little boys shuffled across the green to church school, dragging their satchels behind them. A choirister in a cassock walked by and the splash of red across a Lincoln green was very pleasing to the eye. Tinley's Cafe nearby, with its black frontage and striped black and white canopies, was the sort of place you frequent with your shades and your sun tan and your soft-topped lipstick red TR7. Tea was 45p per person, which explained a lot!

Touring south of Exeter I cycled for about twelve miles and came to Dawlish. A stream flowed through the centre of town over a series of weirs and in Dawlish the ducks swam upstream if they could away from a cloudy sea. The town is very pleasant if you like fairy grottos, twee brick walls and seasonal shrubbery which marks the name of the town. There was a wishing well next to the stream and people would happily toss a few pennies into the bottom. The town drunk could then scale

Clovelly

The day started in style with Mrs Goaman's breakfast special. Eggs and bacon with crispy fried bread. My usual intake of shredded wheat was sadly replaced by rice crispies but the milk was creamy and straight from the cow. Then I had to get on the bike and on with the days work.

In a Hay Field on The Chepstow Road

The hill out of Lynmouth was 1 in 5 for half a mile and 1 in 8 for a further mile. I breathed so hard going up that my lungs hurt for the rest of the day. Sitting in a hay field Barry cooked a failure. Hamburgers and cold sausages and I don't feel hungary at all.

After the riding ends for the day I feel great, hyped up by the exhilarations of enormous amounts of physical exercise. As soon as I stop I shower, or not as when in a field and eat. After an hour, I can barely stand up and my eyes are unable to focus. Thoughts start to disconnect and tend towards a certain surreality. Above, the clouds are tinted with the end of a long summery day and they simmer across the sky silver like. So a deep azure blue replaces the days haze and in the field everything turns to silhouette. The lads clear up the cooking utensils. In a few minutes I'll be in bed. It's 10.10 p.m. and already it grows dark and I long for the faraway feel high in the western highlands of Scotland.

Day 18

Clovelly – Chepstow.

On the road
— Literally!

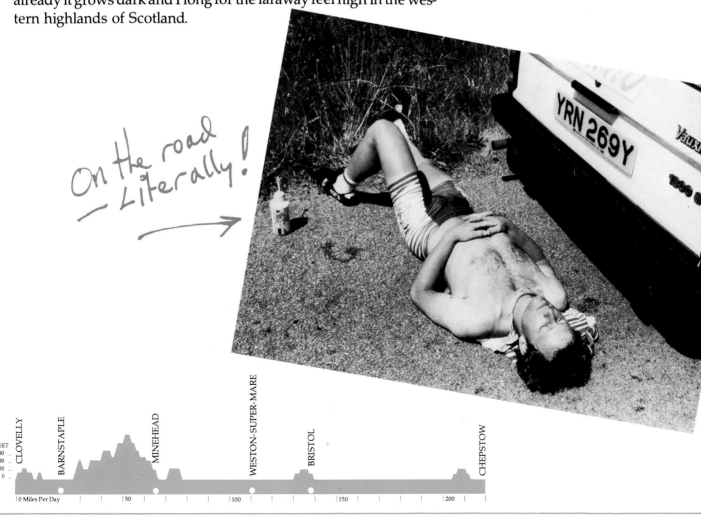

'Breezy flowers seated in blue boats and white boots which any nose may ravage with impunity'.

78

Clovelly and B & B at Mrs Reasgib's.

down and purloin a few bob. On a good night he could maintain complete inebriation – at least his wishes came true. People stand by the well and close their eyes tight. "Please, I wish for lots of money; lots of friends; a fast car; I want to be beautiful". And in goes another few coppers with a clink.

Within half an hour I'd made it to Teignmouth. The busy road followed the railway line and the railway line followed the edge of the sea. Perhaps it was the cloud-blanketed sky which made the sea look flat and grey. Maybe it was the sea that made Teignmouth look dull and weary. Or was it the town itself that gave those mighty frenetic breakers a look of fatigue and loathing, dreading even to lap at the shore?

Just off the main Paignton to Brixham road I stopped the night at a little bed and breakfast called Windyridge House. It had a white-washed front with trim, blue-edged window sills. A sign said 'Vacancies' but unless you agreed to stay the landlady wouldn't tell you the price for the night. Mrs Thrumpwood was a healthy, white-haired, old lady and she served pots of steaming tea for 25p on a plastic lace table cloth which she said was easy to clean. Dotted on top of heavy, ugly sideboards were hand-painted photographs of Mrs Thrumpwood and her late husband. A silver-plated sugar bucket sat next to a pendulum clock gently ticking to and fro. This little living room was just how I imagined the 1940's to be, where clinched waists and padded shoulders would 'click click' in high-heeled shoes, with silk stockings bearing a slightly crooked seam.

Mrs Thrumpwood came in to serve more tea and scones. If I were a child I'd switch on the radio for 'Listen With Mother' and lovely BBC names like Daphne Oxenford and Uncle Ben. As I buttered my scones and looked out of the window I could see a wood, wrecked and littered with fallen trees. My lovely Devon landlady stoked the fire as night was beginning to fall and I felt like an Ovaltinie.

"Have you got enough tea, my dear"? she asked.

"Oh yes, thank you very much", I said. And a burning hot ember fell onto the grate.

The following morning I set off for Brixham. Mrs Thrumpwood had been very accommodating, but she was forthright and suspicious and glad, I think, to see me go. Tourists seem to be a necessary encumbrance to the life of the coast. Once watered, fed and put into bed we're moved on to new pastures. Moved on to look at quaint little harbours or tumble-down houses without doing anything original all day. So, amongst the rolling country lanes amidst ten foot high hedgerows, I put on my nosebag, hoping to reach Brixham later in the morning.

Brixham was one of England's major fishing ports in the Middle Ages. Narrow, cobbled streets are squeezed between old world buildings and everything seems to descend to the harbour. The focal point of the harbour is a full size replica of the Golden Hinde, the surprisingly small ship in which Sir Francis Drake sailed around the world – because it was there! And just a tinkle and clunk away, an amusement arcade vibrated harmlessly as newly weds argued outside. He wanted to play on the machines, she didn't. He stormed off, she relented, she offered to pay, and they went in and carried on with the game.

Next door, the town Aquarium, resplendent in its green-painted brickwork and black, boarded up windows, was reminiscent of a dirty bookshop. Surely not in a little place like Brixham? And as the colours of the boats in the harbour mingled with a sunny day, time became pregnant. For some, time has no meaning except that each day seems to take such a long time to pass, like waiting for the baby that never seems to come. A boy of 14 or 15 staggered over to a group of girls. He jibbered inanely and they pushed him away. His leather jacket was shredded and chained, and his short, spikey hair was bright pink – too much peroxide and it was falling out at the front. He stumbled over to the harbour to urinate over the side. To say how sorry I felt for him is, in real terms, of little consequence.

The outskirts of Plymouth were ugly and dull, a sad disappointment in such a heartland of beauty where one expects unadulterated paradise. Torbay and Teignmouth had prepared me well for this sprawling city at the bottom of Britain, they too were noisy and frenetic.

The next day I cycled across the wild hedgerowed tracts of Bodmin Moor to North Cornwall. I didn't feel like cycling all the way to Land's End. Besides which, the myth of King Arthur exuded from windswept plateaux and crystal caves, from Uther Pendragon and Merlin the Magician.

Everything in Tintagel is either old or related to the legend of Arthur. Ye Olde Originale Shoppe sells Arthur teatowels and Merlin's Magic Honey. Further down the main street, past the old 14th century post office, Guinevere the donkey stood unmoving in a field of dockleaves.

Leaving the street I pushed my bike along a ravine to a small cliff at the top. Past the wooden hut selling tickets and literature I sat on the castle wall. On a dull and windy day the sea pounded on the rocks below. The sea is air and the air is sea and in the crevasses of the stones of Tintagel white and purple thrift smells like softboiled sweets. Tennyson offered his description of Arthur's birth.

On a dismal night in which the bounds of heaven and earth were lost, a dragon-shaped ship shone bright with people on her decks. Gone as soon as seen, Merlin dropped to the cove and watched the great sea fall. Wave after wave, each mightier than the last, 'til at last a ninth one was aflame and roared up to deliver a babe at Merlin's feet. "The King! Here is an heir for Uther"! And as he spoke all at once around him rose in fire 'til presently there followed a calm and free sky and stars.

Dusk settled on smooth faced pebbles rounded in sultry Clovelly bay. Like an English garden, rambling yet precisely so, the whitewashed cottages seem to be governed by the Council of Pretty Places. People peer into the windows of aggrieved tenants as children would into a doll's house. As the occasional soapy smell of freshly laundered washing drifted in the air I fully expected little Noddy to drive down the cobbled lane to the little harbour. Perhaps he'd run over one of the fat cats of Clovelly, who slumped everywhere, jampacked with Devon clotted cream.

"There used to be cannibals here, you know", said Mrs Reasgib, at the bed and breakfast where I was lodging on the outskirts of the village. "A family lived in a forest and anyone who entered it never came out". The wind blew against the bullseye windows, the cloudy sky darkened and the trees rustled. "One day a couple went into the forest and were eaten, funny that, in't it"? Mrs Reasgib offered me a cup of tea, straightened her cardy and went on about King John routing out the forest dwellers and the horrors within. "They cut bits off, didn't they, bits off the men".

"Bits"? I said.

"Yes, bits, you know, *bits*", she looked down at her feet, "and then they killed them".

The living room was richly decorated with

The Wayfarers Cafe on the Chepstow Road

Breakfast is a cup of milky coffee and sugar coated bun, always good anti-bonk medicine. The boy serving me the coffee is nervous at 7.00 a.m. as he spills my coffee all over the counter. The lads will be fast asleep in the hayfield and here the lorry drivers get stuck into their morning bacon butties and tea. I feel great today, maybe something to do with the fact that the finish is in sight and at last I've got my rhythm back. Rhythm and pace are so essential one lapse of concentration and they're gone. Sometimes I feel like an early morning worker just like the rest of the world. But then the wonderful feeling of pedalling free as a bird hits me just occasionally and it makes all the lows, the anguish, insecurity and loneliness all the more worthwhile. The lad at the counter doles out sausage and mash and everyone reads the Daily Mirror. People give me an occasional glance not sure whether to ask an interested question or laugh and I get up and leave.

Mumbles

Just finished my third two hour broadcast with Piccadilly Radio in Swansea. Every day I see two or three radio stations, a newspaper or two and occasionally T.V. Sometimes living on such an emotional knife edge as journeys like this dictate, I feel very close to tears. All my fears are compounded out of nothing. All the major intangibles coagulate into a seething mass. The team are relaxing too much leaving me to flounder a little. I pass off 220 miles in the hills in the wind as nothing and I can't do that any longer. But I can't expect from other people the enormous demands I place upon myself. I told them I needed to be alone. I'll meet them at the hotel in Saundersfoot.

St. Bride's Hotel Saundersfoot

Such a lovely hotel to relax in after a long day. Feel a bit better now but the day has taken its toll. The wind was against me from Swanage onwards and the press stops destroy any rhythm I had.

Chepstow – Saundersfoot.

Live from Swansea, 'Sweeny', Me, and DR Jelty's 'Make-Me-Go-Fast' -Mixture

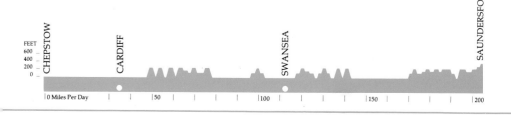

red flock wall covering, a gold floral Axminster and a leather-covered Chesterfield sofa. A copy of the Hartington Times was on the piano stool, opened at the 'Births' column. "I am happy to include a mention of the arrival of a son for Valerie and Andrew Shillibeer at Rollington Cottage, Chisworthy. Master Byron William is the first grandchild to perpetuate an unusual family trait, he has six toes on his left foot".

The next day on the moor road to Barnstable I stopped beside a clump of wild primroses to watch a hairy caterpillar walk across the road. Every stone was a little hill and the only smooth bit was the white line in the centre of the road. A number of cars passed, blowing him over, and each time missing him by inches; each time he'd try again. I wanted to plonk him on my notepad and place him back in the hedgerow, but if he wanted to get to the opposite field at the expense of being flattened, who was I to stop him trying? Like grasshoppers that throw themselves into camp fire flames to crackle in the African Savanna, all little beasties on the move live perilously on the edge of imminent doom. A hump-backed Morris Minor missed him by a whisker, at which he eventually turned back to chomp at a dockleaf. Perhaps he'd try again later in the afternoon.

As I was pushing my bike along the road leading out of Barnstable, an old man with a grey, bushy beard and white Panama hat

passed me by. I quickened my step and caught him up for a chat. He had very baggy eyes, flabby lips and cheeks which sagged to his chin. His nose was red and bulbous, whilst his ears stuck out to catch the wind. With his white canvas bag slung over his shoulder, he walked with resolute determination.

"Can I walk with you a few minutes"? I asked.

He pointed to his ear and fumbled around in his breast pocket for a switch.

"Can I talk to you a while"?

"What yer sayin'"?

"Can I talk to . . ."

"Talk to me"?

"Yes".

"No".

He switched off his hearing aid and carried on. I pulled out my camera.

"Can I . . ."

"No yer don't. I'm not Father Christmas . . . bogger off . . ." and with that, he carried on walking.

So one could say Minehead was a disaster and Weston-Super-Mare all windblown sand and rattling bus shelters. That all old men in white Panama hats are mad and caterpillars that try to cross the road are foolhardy. Travel then becomes a pastiche of life, verging from the slightly exotic to the faintly ridiculous.

Sitting in 'Le Grande Cafe' on the Bristol wharf I could see trendy French shops decked in continental livery. 'Vins Fin' and the grand piano, piped music from Edith Piaf and lukewarm water with a teabag thrown in for good measure. Mock stage-prop places like this are all wicker basket chairs and rubber plants, the décor manufactured instantly to please.

Outside, the carefully manicured cobbles echo the clip-clop of passing footfalls. Floating near the quay urban swans are grey. Living in a city has likewise compromised their pride as they scavenge in the way swans are not wont to do.

As I crossed the bridge over the River Wye, Chepstow Castle looked like a sleeping lion. Built by a Norman general called Strongbow, the castle huddles next to the town whose cramped streets twist up and down the hill. The town centre is Beaufort Square and a series of steps edged around a memorial dedicated to the fallen of the Second World War. The boys and girls of Chepstow sat on the steps scrutinising newcomers in an air of claustrophobia. An old man tripped and stumbled and an innocent youth laughed, not thinking for a moment that one day he too will grow old. Yet Chepstow is clean-looking. Even the punks are well dressed here, the token bleaching and coloured hair being no doubt a disgrace to true punkhood. A fellow walked past with a girl, his cut-off shirt sleeves showing off a tatoo. His earring glinted in the sun as a packet of cigarettes bulged in his back pocket.

Cycling along the Chepstow valley was very pleasant and I didn't stop until I reached Cardiff. With its handsome City Hall, Law Courts and the National Museum of Wales, Cardiff has an impressive city centre. The capital of Wales was a diamond amidst a coastline not noted for its natural beauty, and from Cardiff until Swansea it got steadily worse.

Perhaps there is nothing worse than Port Talbot in the pouring rain. I doubt if even the inhabitants disagree. Yet on a flyover I looked down on the square patchwork jungle of back to back houses and recognised one of the nicest sights of the journey. Red chequered tablecloths flapped alongside sunny yellow dresses. Port Talbot wives chatted over fences, waving to each other half a dozen houses away. Every little square back yard had a shed and a bike and occasionally the fluttering of a pigeon loft.

Stuck on slagheaps and rubble with a refinery for a horizon, the aesthetics were appalling, yet I don't think the strongly-knit community in their colourful backyards cared what other people thought.

"If South Wales is the backside of Britain", a Swansea policeman told me, "then Swansea was its piles". It was raining and the Express Cafe opposite the station served tea that tasted of old socks. Sitting next to the window a frail old lady was wrapped in a chunky-knit pink shawl. Her cheeks were round and rosy but her hands were contorted with arthritis. Her lips were pursed and grey hair fell over her face rather girlishly. She didn't trust the people of Swansea, but then she was from the valley which, she said, housed the friendliest people in the world. "The beauty of Swansea begins and ends at the Guildhall", she said, "the rest is mere ashes to the wind, my dear".

Between Swansea and North Wales the only glimmer of excitement was Frank and his bright orange plastic Unigate milk crate in Aberystwyth. Every day he would stand on his box opposite Woolworth's on the High Street and read quietly from the *Penguin Book of Zen Stories*.

Camarthen 12.00 p.m.

It was very pleasant cycling around St. David's Head and I've made good progress on schedule today. Even though I went to bed late last night, the hotel was very relaxing. Although sitting in a cafe in the High Street I keep nodding off. I'll have to go and find a bench somewhere so I can have a quick snooze.

On the Way to Aberystwyth

the realisation that I am going to make the journey on schedule has just occurred to me. Isn't it strange that in a telephone box in Llangannog I've got a really good feeling particularly as I have only two days to go.

The Tynny Cornel Hotel Talyllyn

Had to come slightly inland to a smashing hotel south of Dolgellau. The proprietor really fed us up. Ham and banana mornay, a thick steak with loads of veg. Pudding was Norwegian Chocolate Cream and strawberry cream cake, lovely. If I ate like this every night it would take me 220 days to get around Britain and I'd weigh in at 14 stone, what a way to go.

Day 20

Saundersfoot – Talyllyn.

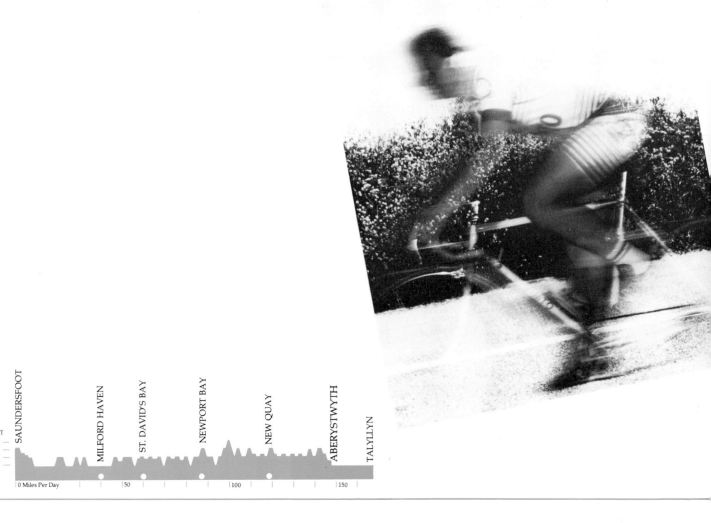

85

"Do you mind if I listen"? I asked as Frank looked down at me from his box.

"Why should I mind"? he replied.

"Only being courteous".

"I hate courtesy and pleasantries. Why don't you say what you mean"?

I thought for a moment as shoppers passed by quite oblivious to this grey haired, middle-aged enlightened being. "Why do you stand on a box"?

"Why do you ride a bike"?

"To get me around the country. You can't get far on a box".

He stopped reading his book and looked down at me, benignly. "I don't need to go anywhere, the world comes past me". He waved his arms in a grand gesture to include the scurrying crowds rushing past. Turning back to

his book he read to me "Once you know the taste of emptiness, you have known the very meaning of life. Carry emptiness, drop the pail of water which is your ego, and your mind and your thoughts, and remember; no water, no moon – emptiness in the hand".

"I once read something by a Zen master, I said, and his face took on a glazed expression as if to say "what, you"?

"Twas climbing up a rubber tree a soft and slimy toad
Did eat a pound of marzipan and dressed himself in woad
'Tis nice' he said 'up here' he said 'so high above the ground
I think I'll try a cloud next time and then the speed of sound"

The Piggly Wiggly Cafe in Dolgellau overlooked Eldon Square which ponged of slain lambs and bone marrow. The cafe advertised hot doughnuts at 10p each and George the proprieter served them up with gusto.

"Lovely cafe you've got", I said.

"Happy cafe, that's me", said George. "Three doughnuts", he said to three girls sitting in the corner, "and mind what you do with the holes".

The girls were as ordinary as some girls appear to be and as they munched and slurped they talked. "Graham never put bubbly bath in so I had to breath in 'cos you can see", she had widely spaced eyes and an adolescent acne spot on both cheeks. "I'm not happy with my bum, but Graham says he likes all of me so that's put my mind at rest".

The girl talk went on and a seagull squalked in the square. The other girl was conscious of her big nose and a third had a lisp. "Audrey alwaith dithapearth at the latht danth, don't you Audrey, you know if she doethn't fanthy any-one", and at the expense of little fat Audrey the two girls laughed.

Crossing the Lleyn Peninsular from Porthmadog I arrived in Caernarfon and found a small cafe behind the castle. With her tweed checked blouson and grey pleated skirt, Caernarfon seemed quite a traditional town. The North Welsh coast was headscarfed on this cold and blustery day. The cafe's dining area was square and cosy with a mock wood pillar supporting the ceiling from the centre of the room. The waitress in her regulation blue chec-ked apron brought me tea and toasted tea cakes. Munching and slurping, it occured to me that this was the 241st cafe I had visited on the journey!

Bangor High Street seemed less commercial than Caernarfon, more human, more liveable. People walked up and down incessantly, doing their Saturday shopping. A group of gospel singers told me that Jesus was going to save me and I cycled past Conway and then on to the loveliness of Llandudno.

Llandudno looked like a frock-coated Victorian gentleman escorting his wasp-waisted lady along the broad promenade. The elegant bow windows and balconied hotels were still there after a century of fashionable gentility. I imagined this as a haven for Harris Tweed Norfolk-jacketed explorers. Sir Henry Morton Stanley, Livingstone's great contemporary, would surely have favoured the translucent sea breeze.

On the way to the brisk tawdriness of Abergele the signs said 'Welcome to Belgrano Village' and 'This Way to Winkie's Bingo', and the air tasted of broken-off bits of candyfloss drifting in the wind.

Rhyl was bursting at the seams with people intent on enjoying themselves, and it looked as if they were. In Prestatyn the Council of Very Sedate People was determined to keep the gawdy hamburger trippers away. The sand-blown sea front culled the crowds as the occasional solitary soul took the dog for a walk. After the industrial quagmire of Connah's Quay and Queensferry, the end of the journey was close at hand and I cut across the Wirral to Liverpool.

Day 21

Left the hotel early. Biked onto Barmouth and through Porthmadog. Porthmadog seemed a bit better in the summer season than when I was last there. Instead of a cold wind cricket bats stand in baskets outside newsagents and shell shaped pieces are piled in cellophane covered dishes. On past Criccieth and then Caernarvon.

The Bell Tower Cafe

I remember last time I was here wondering how I'd feel getting here now. It's a relief to have got here again. All sorts of places are landmarks for the final few miles before the finish. As I sat down for a coffee the same waitress came up to me having remembered me from winter. She still had thick ankles but she was one of the the most beautiful ladies I'd seen on the journey.

The Chequers Hotel Northophall

I can't understand why after 250 miles I don't feel tired. Maybe my form is becoming very good, maybe it's the exhaustion of the penultimate day. All of a sudden the journey is virtually over and another expedition ends. I can't say I'm glad.

Hayfields seem so far away as I sit in the dining room of the Chequers. Buttered mushrooms cooked in stilton cheese and red wine followed by fillet steak and black forest gateau. Makes a nice change from peanut butter and jam sandwiches. After blasting around Anglesey I rode from Bangor to Northophall averaging 26 mph. It was nice to see all the glitter and gloss of Rhyl. Everybody seemed to be having a good time. Bingo was in full swing.

And as everything seems to be in and out of sequence, a whole series of non sequetors I lose concentration at the end of the day. I think of Plymouth, Eastbourne, Boston anywhere. I think hard, where am I now, where am I going and where did I want to go? How thoughts become timeworn .

Talyllyn – Northophall.

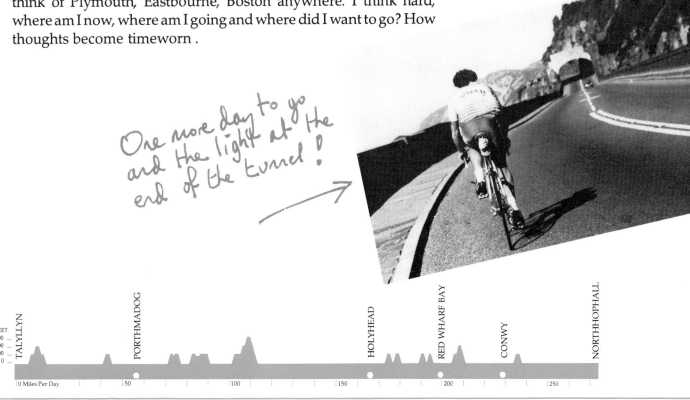

One more day to go and the light at the end of the tunnel!

FEET
600
400
200
0

TALYLLYN — PORTHMADOG — HOLYHEAD — RED WHARF BAY — CONWY — NORTHHOPHALL

0 Miles Per Day   50   100   150   200   250

"Liverpool Lou, love, my Liverpool Lou.
Why don't you behave like other girls do.
Oh why does my poor heart keep following you.
Just stay home and love me like other girls do."

Tourists start early in Liverpool, they've come to look at inner city decay. A 'Schwarzreisen Happy Tour' bus deposits a large group of Austrians by the Catholic Cathedral, led by a guide and a young boy in lederhosen holding a red and white flag on a stick. "Ze roof es leaking" said the guide and everyone leaned back and looked up.

Liverpool has two cathedrals, and from the space age Catholic cathedral you can see the Anglican version which looks like a coal-fired power station. Originally intended to be larger than St Peter's in Rome, this bomb-proof mountain of red brick overlooks the skyline of Liverpool below.

As I cycled down to Pierhead via Bold Street and St James Street one of the famous Mersey ferries smoked and chugged into dock. Gulls squealed and scavanged on the remains of last night's fish and chip wrappers as the aged and unemployed sat on steel benches gazing out across the river. As the Liver Building clock chimed a quarter to eleven the yellow cranes of Cammell-Laird were motionless and the ferry set sail yet again. From here Birkenhead looked dark red and grey, the oily stain of bygone days rusty and still.

"There used to be ocean liners here, you know", said a man standing next to me, "and there was seven miles of dock between Garston and Seaforth". He paused and looked sad, "It's all gone now, Liverpool's all gone now. Everybody's got greedy, they all want the boss's share. It's the trade unions, they should do as the men tell them, not the other way round. The bosses have big cars and houses in the country, and what happens to the rest of us . . .". Another ferry came and went and the clock struck twelve as he walked away.

Down the stairs a whiff of Friday night excrement hit the air and I pushed my bike up St James' Street again to Williamson Square and a drink in the Queen's Arms. There was a heavy thick air, the bar tops were marble and the ballustrade was mahogany. The floor was thickly carpeted and engraved mirrors reflected stubbly men with hollow cheeks. On the wall a host of black and white photographs of actors curled and peeled.

"They're all fir coat and no drawers them", said one chap downing his third pint of Higsons. "Be livin' in Formby next, actors are all the same, all mouth and rumpy pumpy", he placed his glass on the table with a thump, "avva birra Grace Kelly meself when I get home to see the missus", he chuckled and got up and left.

Outside a clown was attempting the first solo tightrope walk across Church Street. A crowd gathered and the newspaper vendor on the corner wasn't selling any papers. Every now and then he would undo his shoelaces and retie them again. Tarnished and torn on the corner of the violet-coloured Playhouse he was hooked to distraction on unfiltered Woodbine cigarettes.

Walking along the Bold Street precinct a couple of banjo players were singing their hearts out. There were hamburger stalls and well-dressed folk and people who passed by for fun and the chorus remained the same, " . . . swimming pools, movie stars, Maggie Thatcher — boo . . .".

They had a happy, tousle-haired countenance did Berni and Pat the banjo players from Salford. "Liverpool is the greatest city in the world", said Berni. "I've lived in 'Frisco, New York, L.A. and Liverpool is the best. It's the atmosphere, the essence of friendly, smiling people. In Manchester they've all got long faces and on Market Street it's unbearable".

There was a shout from the other side of the precinct from a man selling red cherries. "Will you shud up, you're getting on me nerves".

I went over to buy some cherries as Berni played 'Liverpool Lou'. "They're not that bad are they"? I ventured, "at least it's free".

"Not bad! They get on yer flamin' nerves, all day the same old stuff. Tell 'em they can 'ave some of me cherries if they shud up", he scowled.

I liked Liverpool, I marvelled at its vitality and was in awe of a once highly fashionable city. I liked the humour and the optimism, the bare-faced cheek, the cocky spirit, and the healthy disregard for authority. Then there was the intrinsic defiance of the people. Yet for the defiance to be effective it has to be more far reaching than the trajectory of a hand-thrown brick. Out of the corner of the eye, Myrtle Street in Toxteth looks hollow and drawn. The hand-thrown brick lies waiting in the street, strewn as in battle. The boarded windows are daubed with the frustration of a forgotten tribe. Sitting on a brick wall in Myrtle Street I decided the journey must end. Two little girls sat next to me, one wearing a red hat. She was a beautiful little girl, toughened on the streets.

So at the end of another journey imaginary processes begin to take over. Clockwork dreams remind you of the adventure, ensuring you don't forget. But there is always the nuance or the moment that disappears for good however hard you try. Mr Fairbairns Voodoo Lilies will shortly perish and droop and Auntie Annie's clocks will always rest at 13½ minutes to six. Detail of everything else will be relegated into the farflung recesses of imperfect memory. Then all of a sudden on a distant shore or a mountain top far away, I'll think of Mr Grimshaw sitting under his banyan tree watching the pageant of life go by.

On the way to the end of the journey

Looking forward immensely to the finish in Blackpool. I feel happy and sad. Happy in that the aching and desperate fatigue will very soon stop. Sad because I enjoy it. As I leave the hotel before chirping birds wake up I know now how much this trip has meant to me. Just like so many things the journey had little worth in its intrinsic concept but it had to be done whatever. It wasn't the doing but the realisation that having done it I shouldn't have to consider it any more. Journeys like this are really acts of evolution and go around in circles, very slowly. Much further than 228 miles a day.

Liverpool 11.30 a.m.

Having emerged from the Wirral, Liverpool is the last city before the end. Ian and Barry were waiting for me at the Liver building and we carried on to Southport. A few people waved, I suppose the odd person might know what I was doing. Five minutes later I just became another mad memory.

In sight of the Tower

The Tower in view as is the crowd. Doctor Jelly and his Celebrated Verandah Band play some stirring stuff and I raise my arms as I cross the line, People who don't know me wish me well and I wonder how much the British love a conquering hero, people can be so nice when they're given something to cheer about. The band play, the end of the journey, a kiss from a beautiful girl. And from the crowd out comes my Dad to give me a hug. My cycling round the world was a difficult thing for him to appreciate. But this time I knew he understood.

Day 22

Northophall – Blackpool.

I've made it at last!

The Mayor of Blackpool and lovely Tracy 'Queen of the lights'!

All men dream: but not equally. Those who dream by night in the dusty recesses of their minds wake in the day to find that it was vanity: but the dreamers of the day are dangerous men, for they may act their dream with open eyes, to make it possible. (Seven Pillars of Wisdom, Ch. 1) T.E. LAWRENCE.

COASTAL CYCLING RECORD BROKEN

The record for cycling 5,500 miles round the coast of Britain was broken yesterday by Nick Sanders, 26, from Glossop, Derbyshire, who completed it in 22 days and four hours.

When he arrived back at his starting point, Blackpool Tower, he had comfortably broken the previous record—142 days—set five years ago.

NIck pedals into the record books

CYCLIST Nick Sanders made a truimphant return to Blackpool this week after pedalling an incredible 5,500 miles around the coast of Britain in a record breaking 22 days.

Nick, from Gloss Derbyshire, set off Blackpool tower on 10 determined to se new world recor for the aro distance

And o volved a ca Ni

He's made it! Nick breaks world record

GLOSSOP cyclist Nick Sanders claimed another place in the Guinness Book of Records on Sunday when he completed his round Britain ride. And after 5,532 miles of coastal cycling behim, he still managed ile as he crossed the line in Blackpool schedule.

ayor of Blackpool nd to give Nick an elcome before he mped by well-had gathered famous

"22 Days Around the of Britain" — will be lished in September.

There were some ing moments on th Nick said on Wedr "I did not hear it,

elly an d

Super biker smashes a world record

By REG LITTLE

SUPER-cyclist Nick Sanders raced into Blackpool yesterday to smash a world record.

Nick completed a staggering 5,500-mile trip around Britain's coastline in just 22 days.

Hundreds of well-wishers cheered him on along a breezy Blackpool promenade

where also be

Waitin was Black cillor Cyril Lowe and Queen of Lights, Tracey Murtagh.

"It's been a fabulous trip," said Nick, who had to pedal 17 hours a day to hack the old 165-day record dow 22 days.

"The har last

JOURNEY TO THE SOURCE OF THE NILE

NICK SANDERS

Available in hardback and softback.